Joan's Goat

Words by Amanda Graham
Illustrated by Greg Holfeld

Joan had a goat,
a silly, silly goat.

"Whoa!" said Joan.
"Don't eat my toast."

But the goat ate the toast, so Joan moved the goat.

"Whoa!" said Joan. "Don't eat my coat."

But the goat ate the coat, so Joan moved the goat.

"Whoa!" said Joan. "Don't eat my soap."

But the goat ate the soap.

"That's it," said Joan. "No more goat!"

So she took the goat afloat in her little green boat.

"Whoa!" said Joan.
"Don't eat my boat."

Joan had a goat,
a silly, silly goat.